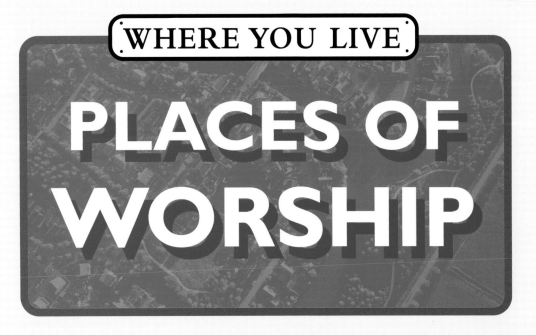

WHERE YOU LIVE

PLACES OF WORSHIP

Ruth Nason

Photography by Chris Fairclough

W
FRANKLIN WATTS
LONDON • SYDNEY

First published in 2007 by
Franklin Watts
338 Euston Road
London NW1 3BH

Franklin Watts Australia
Level 17/207 Kent Street
Sydney NSW 2000

ISBN 978 0 7496 7176 1

Dewey classification number: 726

A CIP catalogue record for this book is available from the British Library.

Planning and production by Discovery Books Limited
Editor: Paul Humphrey
Designer: Ian Winton
Photography: Chris Fairclough

Printed in China

Franklin Watts is a division of Hachette Children's Books, an Hachette Livre UK company.

Photo acknowledgements
All the photographs in this book were supplied by Chris Fairclough except for the following:
Michael Nason, page 15 (bottom right), John Bristow, page 27.

Note about questions in this book
The books in the Where You Live series feature lots of questions for readers to answer. Many of these are open-ended questions to encourage discussion and many have no single answer. For this reason, no answers to questions are given in the books.

Contents

Places of worship in Britain

A place of worship is a building where people can go to pray. It is also a meeting place for followers of a religion.

- What tells you that this building is a church?
- How many churches are there in your town or village?
- Which places of worship have you been to?

In Britain, the main type of place of worship is a **church**. There are very many churches in the country and in towns.

Places of worship in Britain also include:
- **synagogues** for Jewish people
- **mosques** for Muslims
- **temples** for Hindus or Buddhists
- **gurdwaras** for Sikhs.

WHERE YOU LIVE
Find the list of places of worship in your local telephone directory. Which types are there?

Some places of worship are beautiful buildings, like this Hindu temple in Neasden, London.

Some are very old buildings. They help you to learn about the past.

The children in this picture made a school visit to a mosque. It helped them to understand what Muslims believe and do.

- In what way is the temple above similar to the church on page 6?
- What things do you expect to find inside a place of worship?

Religions in Britain

Britain is a **multicultural** country. People from many different **cultures** and **faiths** live here.

- In the 2001 census, which religion did most people in Britain say they belonged to?

- In your class, which religion do most people belong to?

Every ten years, the government collects information about all the people in Britain. This is called a **census**. One question in the census is: Which religion do you belong to? The pie chart below shows what people said in 2001.

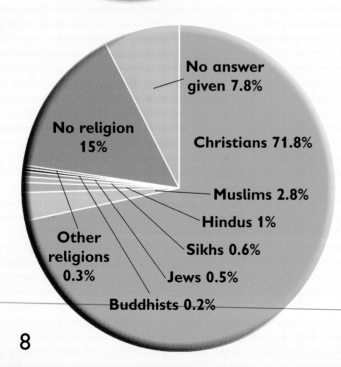

No answer given 7.8%

Christians 71.8%

No religion 15%

Muslims 2.8%

Hindus 1%

Other religions 0.3%

Sikhs 0.6%

Jews 0.5%

Buddhists 0.2%

WHERE YOU LIVE
Do a survey of your class to find which religions you belong to.

8

People in Britain began to be Christians a very long time ago. The other religions were brought to Britain later.

•What shape is the green roof of this mosque?
•On which day of the week do many Muslims go to pray at their mosque?
•When did Muslims begin to build this mosque, by laying the foundation stone?

In the 20th century, many Hindu, Sikh and Muslim people moved to Britain from India, Pakistan and countries in Africa and the Middle East. They have changed some old buildings into temples, gurdwaras and mosques. They have also built brand new places of worship, like this mosque in Luton.

Identifying a place of worship

Places of worship are very special places for the people who go there. They often like to build places that look different from the other buildings around.

People of different religions build places of worship in different styles.

All gurdwaras (below) have one or more orange flags outside. Some gurdwaras have a **dome**.

• Why do you think people want their places of worship to look special?

• Why are many religious buildings large, with tall towers?

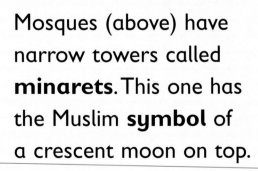

Mosques (above) have narrow towers called **minarets**. This one has the Muslim **symbol** of a crescent moon on top.

Places of worship often have a symbol on the wall outside. This is a Jewish **menorah** on the side of a synagogue (right). The symbol below is used on some Hindu temples.

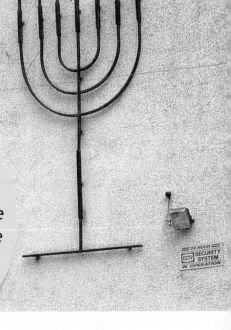

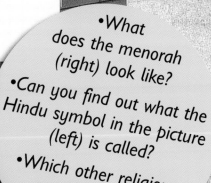

- What does the menorah (right) look like?
- Can you find out what the Hindu symbol in the picture (left) is called?
- Which other religious symbols do you know?

WHERE YOU LIVE
Find the biggest place of worship in your town or village.

Many churches have a tower, like the one on page 10. Some church towers have a pointed **spire** on top. See page 6 for an example.

The building on the left is a type of church building called a **chapel**. It has no tower or spire.

11

Church buildings

Christian **monks** came to the British Isles about 1,600 years ago to tell people about the Christian religion. From then the religion spread all over Britain. Many churches were built. The church on the right was built in **Norman** times.

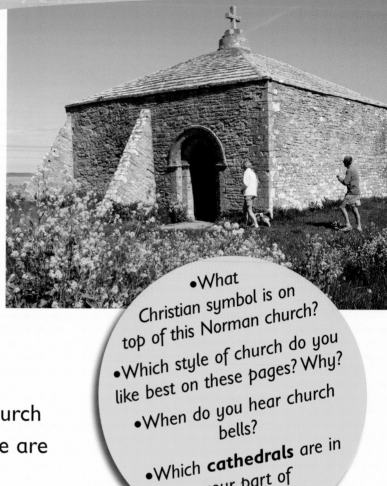

You will find many styles of church buildings in Britain today. Some are modern like the one below.

- What Christian symbol is on top of this Norman church?
- Which style of church do you like best on these pages? Why?
- When do you hear church bells?
- Which **cathedrals** are in your part of Britain?

Church towers were built to hang bells. The bells were rung to tell people that it was time to go to church.

These Jews are going to their main service. It is held at the synagogue every Saturday.

Muslims pray five times every day. They can pray in any place, but on Fridays they try to pray together at the mosque.

- What special clothing do some people wear to show what religion they belong to?
- In your town, which is the day when most people go to their place of worship?

WHERE YOU LIVE
Notice what is different in your town or village on the day that people go to their place of worship.

Special events

People go to their place of worship to celebrate special events in their lives, such as getting married.

- Have you been to a wedding at a place of worship? What do you remember about it?
- Where is the bride in the two pictures on this page?
- What other important events in their lives do people celebrate?

The picture above was taken after a Christian wedding. The picture left shows a Hindu wedding **ceremony**.

People also go to their place of worship to celebrate religious festivals. This picture shows Sikhs at a festival parade.

• Which religious festivals can you think of?
• In the picture below, what do you think the people in the yellow jackets are doing?
• What do you notice about the writing on the float in the parade?

At a festival, people remember an event or a person from the history of their religion. This helps them to think about important ideas from the religion. Many festivals are happy times, with decorations and parties.

WHERE YOU LIVE
Ask someone who belongs to a religion to tell you about their favourite religious festival.

21

A place to meet

Many places of worship have several different rooms as well as the main area where services take place. For example, there may be:

- a hall where a large number of people can meet
- an office
- a kitchen
- rooms that are used by small groups of people, such as members of a club or a class
- a library or resources room
- a coffee lounge or café.

- What do you think happens in the office of a place of worship?
- What type of things do you think people can look at in the resources room of a place of worship?
- Which places of worship in your town have a café?

Gurdwaras have a room called the **langar**. Sikhs cook and share a meal there after every service.

Some rooms at a mosque are used for classes. Children go there to learn to read the Muslim holy book, the Qur'an.

- What questions would you like to ask the girls in this picture?
- Why do people like to be in a choir or music group?

WHERE YOU LIVE
Look for notices outside places of worship that tell you about the activities that people take part in.

Choirs often meet at a church or other place of worship for practice.

Who works there?

At many places of worship there is one main person whose job is to:

- lead prayers and services
- perform ceremonies
- teach people about their religion
- care for people, especially at difficult times.

In some churches a **minister** or **priest** (above right) leads the service.

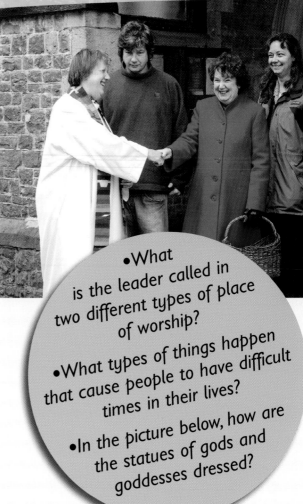

•What is the leader called in two different types of place of worship?

•What types of things happen that cause people to have difficult times in their lives?

•In the picture below, how are the statues of gods and goddesses dressed?

At Friday midday prayers in a mosque the **imam** (left) gives a talk.

A priest (right) performs ceremonies at a Hindu temple. Part of his job is to dress the statues of gods and goddesses. He also makes **offerings** to them.

24

Many places of worship have a caretaker who looks after the building. Some have a secretary and a gardener (right).

Some people work at their place of worship as **volunteers**. This lady (below) takes flowers to people from her church who are not well.

- Which people do you know who work as volunteers?
- What job would you volunteer to do for an organisation that you belong to?

Volunteers also play music for services (below), look after and teach young people and welcome visitors.

WHERE YOU LIVE
Think of some questions to ask the leader of a place of worship.

Helping others

People from all religions believe that they should help others, especially people in need. At their places of worship, they organise activities to help the needy.

For example, twice each week, volunteers at this Hindu temple (below) serve a lunch to local elderly people.

- Who are the needy people in your town?
- What type of help do they need?

Sometimes people from different places of worship do things together. This notice shows how people at a synagogue support the work of a nearby church.

People help the needy in their local **community**. They also raise money and do things to help poor people around the world. These young women from a church in England joined in a project to build houses in Kenya.

WHERE YOU LIVE
Look for local newspaper reports about people at a place of worship helping people in need.

• What activities does your school organise to help people in need?
• Which countries do you know that have many people in need?
• What do you think these young women told their friends about their time in Kenya?

Glossary

Baptised Sprinkled with water, or immersed in water, as part of the ceremony of baptism. This ceremony marks the time when someone becomes a part of the Christian faith.

Bible The holy book of Christians.

Bishop A church leader, in charge of the churches in an area called a diocese.

Buddha The name that was given to the man who discovered and began to teach people the ideas of Buddhism, more than 2,500 years ago.

Cathedral The main church in a district called a diocese. The person in charge of a diocese is a bishop.

Census A count made of all the people who live in a place. At the same time, information is collected by asking everyone to answer the same questions.

Ceremony A set of actions which are carried out in a dignified, serious way, to show that something is important and special.

Chapel A plain church building, with a front that has a triangular shape at the top. Chapels were built by groups of Christians such as Baptists and Methodists. Chapel can also mean a separate area inside a church or cathedral.

Church A building where Christians worship. 'Church' can also mean all the people who belong to the church.

Community All the people who live in a place.

Culture The background, beliefs and ways of life of different groups of people. For example, each country has its own culture.

Dome A curved, roof structure usually hemispherical (half a round ball) in shape.

Faith Belief, or another word for religion.

Font A container for the water that is used in the Christian ceremony of baptism.

Gurdwara A place where Sikhs go to worship. A gurdwara can be just a room or a whole building. The one thing it must have is the Sikh holy book, called the Guru Granth Sahib.

Holy book A book that is used as a guide by the people of a religion. Most holy books were written a long time ago, but people find help in them for their lives today.

Imam The leader of prayers at a mosque.

Langar A large kitchen or dining hall in a gurdwara. People cook and eat a meal together there after a service. 'Langar' also means the food they eat there.

Lectern A reading desk.

Menorah A seven-branched candle holder, often used as a symbol of the Jewish religion.

Minaret A tower at a mosque. In the past, a minaret was built so that a Muslim could call out from the top, five times each day, to tell people when it was time to pray. Minarets in Britain are not all used in this way.

Minister A person who leads worship and performs ceremonies in a church.

Monk A man who has made vows to live by the rules of a particular religious group. Monks live apart from ordinary people, in a monastery.

Mosque A building where Muslims go to pray.

Multicultural Made up of many groups of people with different cultures.

Norman From a period that began in England after 1066, when William the Conqueror became king. He came from Normandy in France.

Offering Gift.

Parson A Christian preacher.

Plaque A metal plate or stone slab fixed, for example, to a wall. The writing on plaques remembers something important.

Priest A person who leads worship and performs ceremonies. The word 'priest' is used by people in some Christian churches and by Hindus.

Respect Admiration and care for something that you believe is special and important.

Service A time when people worship together, including saying or singing prayers, hearing readings from their holy book, and sometimes hearing a talk called a sermon.

Spire A tall cone shape pointing upwards, on top of a church tower.

Stained-glass window A window made from pieces of coloured glass, which are fixed together to make pictures or patterns.

Symbol A simple picture that is used to represent something.

Synagogue A building where Jews meet and worship.

Temple A place of worship. Buddhists, Hindus and others call their places of worship temples. Another name for a Hindu temple is a mandir.

Vicar The leader of an Anglican church. A vicar's house is called a vicarage.

Volunteer A person who does a job for no pay, because he or she wants to help.

Further information

Visiting a place of worship

It's best if you can visit a place of worship with a guide who can tell you what happens there, point out interesting things and answer your questions. But you could also make some visits on the internet.

Useful websites

Virtual tours of all types of places of worship start at **http://re-xs.ucsm.ac.uk/re/places/**

You can tour a Hindu temple in Bradford at **http://www.ngfl.ac.uk/re/shreeprajapati mandir.htm**

You can visit a synagogue, mosque and gurdwara in Wales at **http://www.ngfl-cymru.org.uk/vtc/ngfl/ re/m_parry_carmarthenshire/addoldai /index.html**

You can visit a synagogue, some churches and a mosque, starting from **http://www.hitchams.suffolk.sch.uk/ synagogue/index.htm**

A website with links to pages about different Christian denominations, including their buildings, is at **http://www.request.org.uk/main/ churches/churches.htm**

You can also find out about Christianity at **http://infants.reonline.org.uk/**

Books

The *My Community* series (Franklin Watts) includes books about Hindu, Jewish, Muslim and Sikh people in Britain.

The *My Life, My Religion* series (Franklin Watts) includes books about the leaders of places of worship, such as Anglican Curate, Catholic Priest and Sikh Granthi.

The *Start-Up Religion* series (Evans Publishing) includes books on *Visiting a Church*, *Visiting a Gurdwara*, *Visiting a Mandir*, *Visiting a Mosque* and *Visiting a Synagogue*.

The *Where We Worship* series (Franklin Watts) includes books about the places of worship of each of the six main religions in the world.

Index